Wheels, wings and water

Motorcycles

Heather Miller

Raintree

www.raintreepublishers.co.uk
Visit our website to find out more information about **Raintree** books.

To order:
☎ Phone 44 (0) 1865 888112
▤ Send a fax to 44 (0) 1865 314091
▢ Visit the Heinemann Bookshop at **www.raintreepublishers.co.uk** to browse our catalogue and order online.

First published in Great Britain by Raintree, Halley Court, Jordan Hill, Oxford OX2 8EJ, part of Harcourt Education.
Raintree is a registered trademark of Harcourt Education Ltd.

Editorial: Charlotte Guillain and Diyan Leake
Design: Michelle Lisseter
Picture Research: Maria Joannou and Amor Montes de Oca
Production: Lorraine Hicks

Originated by Dot Gradations
Printed and bound in China by South China Printing Company

ISBN 1 844 21367 6
07 06 05 04 03
10 9 8 7 6 5 4 3 2 1

British Library Cataloguing in Publication Data
Miller, Heather
Motorcycles. – (Wheels, wings and water)
388.3'475
A full catalogue record for this book is available from the British Library.

Acknowledgements
Bruce Coleman, Inc./Frank A. Cara, **8**; Bruce Coleman, Inc./Stephen Kline, **13**; Getty Images/Allsport Concepts, **9**, **23** (mudguard); Getty Images/Imagebank, **16**; Getty Images/Taxi, **15R**, **22**, **24**; Index Stock/Doug Mazell, **15L**; Motorcycle Hall of Fame, **10**, **11**; Rex Features/Stewart Cook, **23** (stunt); Transparencies, Inc./Aaron Stevenson, **6**, **23** (engine); Transparencies, Inc./Jane Faircloth, **4**, **23** (vehicle); TRIP/J. Okwesa, **7**; TRIP/Treanor, **5**, **14**, **23** (brake and handlebars), backcover; Visuals Unlimited/Bruce Gaylord, **18**; Visuals Unlimited/Igna Spence, **17**; Visuals Unlimited/Images Internationals, **20**; Visuals Unlimited/Jeff Greenberg, **12**, backcover; Visuals Unlimited/John D. Cunningham, **21**; Visuals Unlimited/S. K. Patrick, **19**

Cover photograph of motorbikes, reproduced with permission of Robert Harding Picture Library.

Every effort has been made to contact copyright holders of any material reproduced in this book. Any omissions will be rectified in subsequent printings if notice is given to the publishers.

Some words are shown in bold, **like this**. You can find them in the glossary on page 23.

Contents

What are motorcycles?

Motorcycles are **vehicles** with wheels and an **engine**.

Motorcycles can carry people and things.

brake   handlebar

Riders steer with **handlebars**.

They squeeze the **brake** with their hand to stop.

What do motorcycles look like?

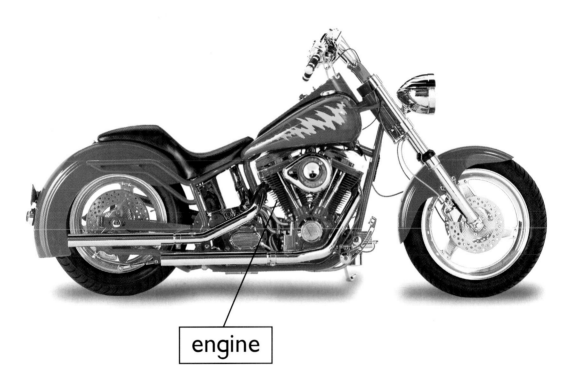

engine

Motorcycles look like bicycles with **engines**.

petrol tank

Motorcycles have **petrol tanks**.

Petrol makes the engine go.

What are motorcycles made of?

chrome

Motorcycles have metal parts.

The shiny metal parts are called chrome.

mudguard

Some motorcycles have plastic parts.

The **mudguards** on this dirt bike are plastic.

How did motorcycles look in the past?

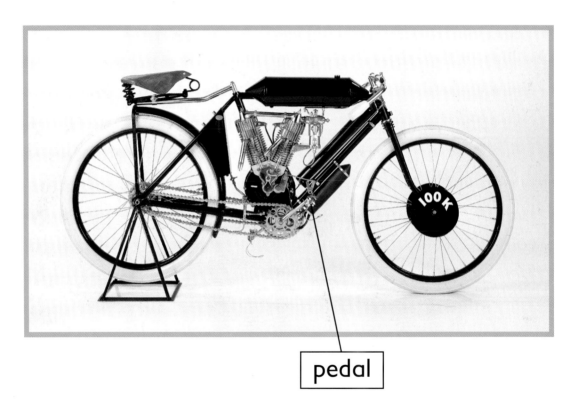

pedal

The first motorcycles looked like bicycles.

Some motorcycles had **pedals**.

tyre

Later, motorcycles were made to go faster.

These motorcycles had larger **engines** and wide rubber tyres.

What is a scooter?

A scooter is a small motorcycle.

Scooters do not go very fast.

Many people in crowded cities ride scooters.

People ride scooters for fun, too.

What is a touring motorcycle?

A touring motorcycle is large.

It is made for going on long trips.

saddlebag

sidecar

Touring motorcycles have saddlebags to carry things.

Some touring motorcycles have sidecars to carry other riders.

15

What is a quad bike?

A quad bike is a motorcycle with four wheels.

Quads can go where there are no roads.

People ride quads in sand and mud.

Some people race their quads.

Some people use quads to do work.

What is a dirt bike?

A dirt bike is a motorcycle used for racing over rough ground.

Dirt bikes can climb hills.

Dirt bikes are lighter than street motorcycles.

Riders can do **stunts** on dirt bikes.

Why are some motorcycles special?

Racing motorcycles go very fast.

They have large **engines**.

Motorcycles can be very small.

Here are some clowns in a parade on their little motorcycles.

Quiz

Do you know what kind of motorcycle this is?

Can you find it in the book?

Look for the answer on page 24.

22

Glossary

brake
handle that can be pushed or squeezed to make something stop

engine
machine that makes a vehicle move

handlebars
part of a bicycle or motorcycle that you hold on to with your hands

mudguard
curved plastic or metal piece above the wheels on a vehicle

pedal
part of a bicycle that you push with your feet to make it move

petrol tank
holder for the liquid that makes the engine in a vehicle go

stunt
an exciting, dangerous or unusual action

vehicle
something that carries people or things from one place to another

Index

Answer to quiz on page 22.
This is a touring motorcycle.

Titles in the Wheels, Wings and Water series include:

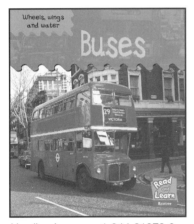

Hardback   1 844 21369 2

Hardback   1 844 21371 4

Hardback   1 844 21366 8

Hardback   1 844 21373 0

Hardback   1 844 21372 2

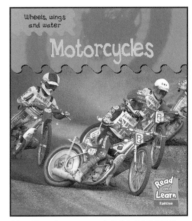

Hardback   1 844 21367 6

Hardback   1 844 21368 4

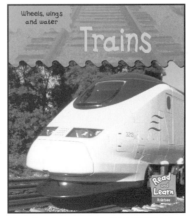

Hardback   1 844 21374 9

Find out about the other titles in this series on our website www.raintreepublishers.co.uk